Tiny Toes Adventures USA

Rafiel Aharoni

Published in Saint Petersburg, FL

Printed in United States

Library of Congress Control Number: [2023916700]

ISBN:

Paperback [979-8-9889547-1-2]

In the heart of NYC, where big dreams arise,
Baby, you'll see skyscrapers touch the skies.
Yellow taxis zoom, and Broadway stars shine bright,
Times Square's neon glow lights up the night.
Central Park's green sprawl, a place to play,
While the Statue of Liberty waves on the bay.
Giggles and coos, as you explore each street,
New York's magic pulse, a baby's heartbeat.

To D.C., little traveler, you now glide,
Past monuments tall, with eyes open wide.
The White House, the Capitol, all in a row,
Cherry blossoms bloom, making hearts glow.
Museums and memories, history's embrace,
Baby's first journey in this grand place.
With each little giggle, a new tale spun,
Washington awaits, let's have some fun!

In Charleston, baby, you will see,
Cobblestone paths and history.
Pastel houses, bright and neat,
Horse-drawn carriages on the street.
Pineapple fountains, water's glee,
Jasmine scents upon the breeze.
Taste the South, its flavors deep,
With every giggle, every leap.
For in this city by the shore,
Baby, you'll discover more!

Miami's sun, so warm and bright,
Tiny toes touch the sand, pure delight!
Palm trees sway, seagulls sing,
Waves whisper tales of oceanic bling.
Tiny shades, a hat so neat,
First time feels, oh, so sweet.
Little traveler, with eyes so wide,
Miami's magic, by the seaside.

In New Orleans, baby, take a peek,
At jazz-filled streets, where trumpets speak.
Mardi Gras beads in colors bright,
French Quarter sights, pure delight!
Gumbo's aroma, beignets sweet,
Dancing feet to a rhythmic beat.
Mississippi's breeze, a soft caress,
Your first NOLA trip, surely the best!

In Chicago, baby, you'll see,
Skyscrapers tall and the glistening sea.
Cloud Gate will shimmer, like a big silver dime,
Windy City's rhythm, a wonderful rhyme.
Stroll in Millennium, under the sun,
Chicago's magic has just begun.
The lake will sparkle, boats bobbing with glee,
Welcome, little traveler, to a city full of spree!

Baby on a journey, to the canyon so deep,
Where colors and shadows in harmony leap.
Echoes of history, tales untold,
Against the grand backdrop, your story unfolds.
Little feet wiggling, under the sun's warm glance,
In this vast wonderland, you've taken your first dance.
With each tiny laugh and curious stare,
You've embraced the Grand Canyon's fresh open air!

In Nashville, baby, take a look around,
Guitar strums and honky-tonk sound.
Bright neon lights dance in the night,
Music City's magic, pure delight.
Tiny cowboy boots tap the floor,
Broadway's rhythm, who could ask for more?
"Batman Building" tall and sleek,
Nashville's wonders, for you to seek.
First time in town, so much to see,
Welcome, little traveler, to Tennessee!

In LA, little traveler, there's much to see,
From Hollywood's sign to the shimmering sea.
Palm trees sway, the sun shines so bright,
City of Angels, in day and at night.
Tiny toes in the sand, a breeze in your hair,
Golden moments, memories to share.
Stroller rides down the boulevard's gleam,
Welcome, baby, to the city of dream!

To San Francisco, baby, you go,
Where the cool winds often blow.
Over Golden Gate, so tall and red,
Dreams of cable cars in your head.
Pier 39, where the sea lions play,
By the bay, you'll dance and sway.
Tiny feet on Lombard's twisty street,
San Fran treats, oh, so sweet!
A city of wonders, sights so grand,
Baby's first adventure in this magical land!

Seattle awaits, with its rain and shine,
Skyscrapers tall, and the waterfront line.
For a baby like you, every sight's a rhyme,
Ferries and fishes, each a wonderful time.

Space Needle points, where the clouds like to play,
Market's bustle, fresh flowers on display.
Tiny hands clapping, in pure child's delight,
Discovering Seattle, what a wondrous sight!

In a stroller through the Strip, Las Vegas lights do gleam,
Neon wonders, sounds abound, it's like a dreamy dream.
Baby headphones on my ears, the world's a gentle song,
With plushy dice in tiny grip, I roll and cruise along.
Casinos grand, and fountains dance, Elvis gives a wink,
This traveling tot's first Vegas jaunt, gone in a blinkety blink!

Little traveler, weary and small,
You've seen the mountains, the cities, them all.
From east to the west, from big to the wee,
Across the vast lands, from sea to sea.
But now, little baby, it's time to rest tight,
Dream of your journeys, as stars shine so bright.
Close those tired eyes, drift into the night,
Home awaits you, everything's just right.

To Carli, my anchor and heart, whose love has been the steadfast light guiding me through every challenge and triumph. Your strength, grace, and unwavering support have been the bedrock upon which this work was built.

To Maverick and Myloh, my remarkable sons, you are both the pulse of my life and the joy in my days. Your laughter, inquisitiveness, and boundless spirits have filled our home with love and have fueled my imagination.

This book, a testament to perseverance and passion, is dedicated to you three – my most cherished treasures. Through its pages, may you always find a reflection of the love I hold for you.

About the Author

Rafiel Aharoni is a writer with a passion for kindling the flames of imagination and curiosity in children. He believes in the power of stories to inspire, teach, and transport young readers into worlds full of adventure and wonder.

While Rafiel currently spends his days studying towards dual degrees in Business Management and Cyber Security, he always finds time to create enchanting tales for his favorite audience: kids. He thrives on the balance between the calculated logic required for his academic pursuits and the wild creativity his writing allows him to express.

Rafiel's journey into the realm of children's literature isn't just driven by his love for storytelling, it's also fueled by his first-hand experiences spending time with children. He knows the value of a good story in lighting up a child's eyes and instilling in them a love for reading.

Although this may be Rafiel's first publication, it is certainly not his last. His work is characterized by a mix of whimsy, humor, and genuine understanding of a child's mind. Each tale he crafts aims to engage, entertain, and educate in equal measure.

When he isn't studying or spinning tales, Rafiel resides in the sunny city of Saint Petersburg, Florida. He believes the state's vibrant natural beauty and diverse culture are the perfect backdrop for dreaming up his next delightful tale.

Rafiel Aharoni: a wonderful father, a great husband, a dedicated student, a doting playmate, and above all, a devoted storyteller for children.

www.ingramcontent.com/pod-product-compliance
Lightning Source LLC
LaVergne TN
LVHW072133070426
835513LV00002B/81